Do You Want to Play?

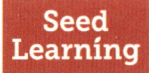
Seed Learning

swing

seesaw

slide

sandbox

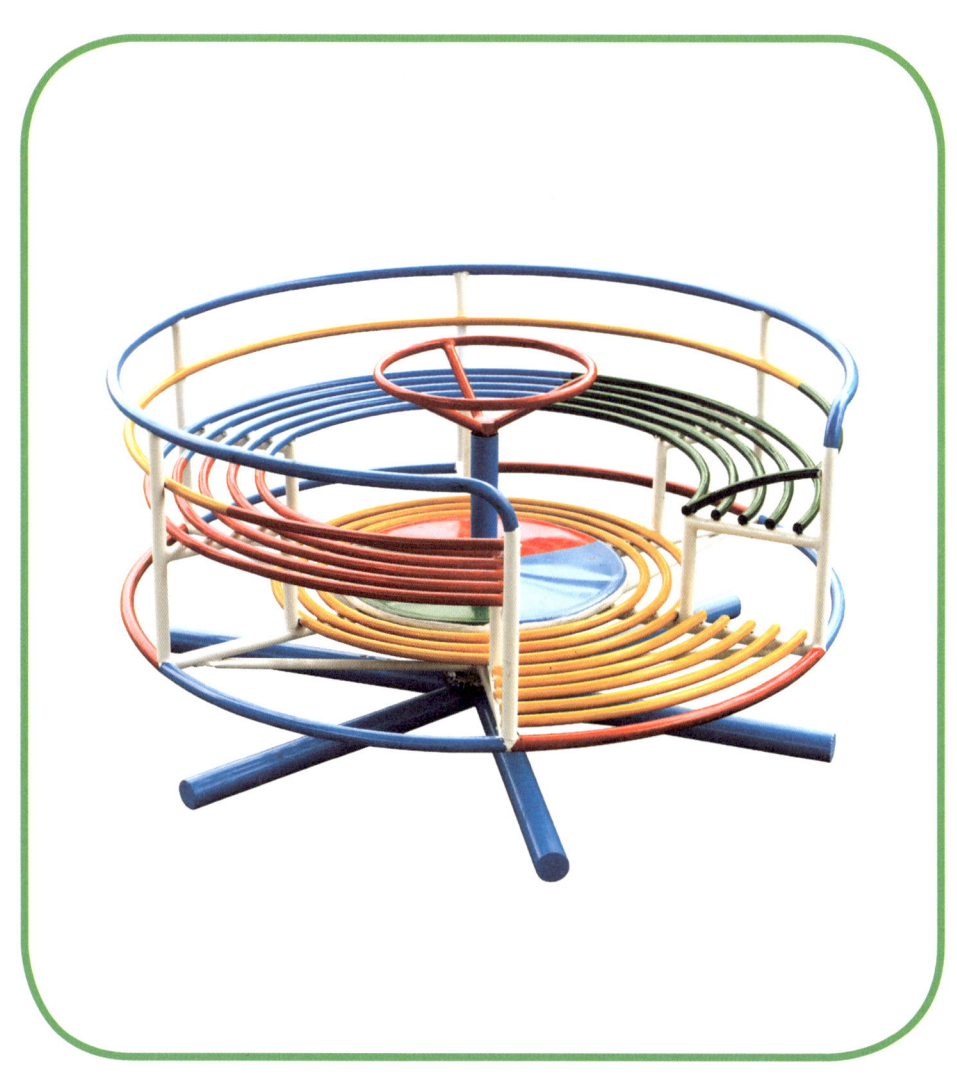

merry-go-round

monkey bars

jungle gym

bench

Do you want to play?

OK. Let's play in the sandbox.

Do you want to play?

OK. Let's play on the seesaw.

Do you want to play?

OK. Let's play on the monkey bars.

Do you want to play?

OK. Let's play on the merry-go-round.

Do you want to play?

OK. Let's play on the jungle gym.

Do you want to play?

No. Let's sit on the bench.

Let's learn about Indonesia.

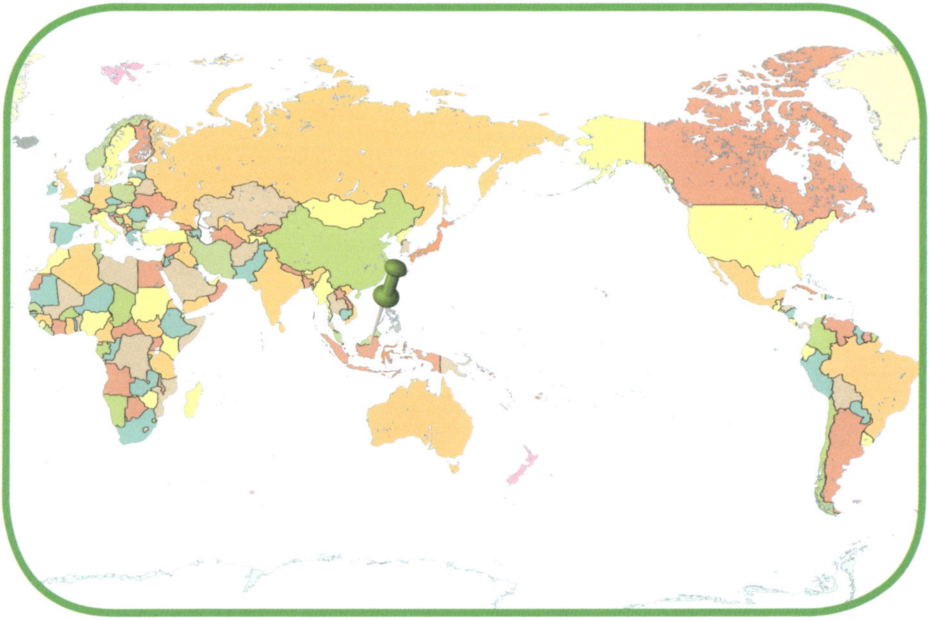

Flag of Indonesia.

Pencak silat